With Eyes of Love

A true story about Alzheimer's for children

Written by Christine Golder
Illustrated by Alison Stevens-Milkins

AuthorHouse™
1663 Liberty Drive
Bloomington, IN 47403
www.authorhouse.com
Phone: 833-262-8899

This book is printed on acid-free paper.

ISBN: 978-1-6655-5020-8 (sc)
ISBN: 978-1-6655-5021-5 (e)

Library of Congress Control Number: 2022901216

Print information available on the last page.

Published by AuthorHouse 03/18/2022

authorHOUSE®

A special thanks to Robin Lombardo
for her encouragement to write
this book for children.

A portion of royalty proceeds will be
donated to the Alzheimer's Research.

My name is Christine. I had a wonderful mother whose name was Emily. She was my best friend. Growing up, my mom and I had so much fun together. She played with me every day.

When I was little she read me stories and nursery rhymes. We took long walks into town to go shopping.

We danced in the basement and roller skated.

We played cards and board games. We would eat candy while we watched T.V. at night.

In the winter, my Mom would build me snow ladies, snow men, snow swans and snow forts. She took me sledding too. We also went ice-skating at Brightwaters lake.

In the summer we'd go swimming for hours in the backyard pool.

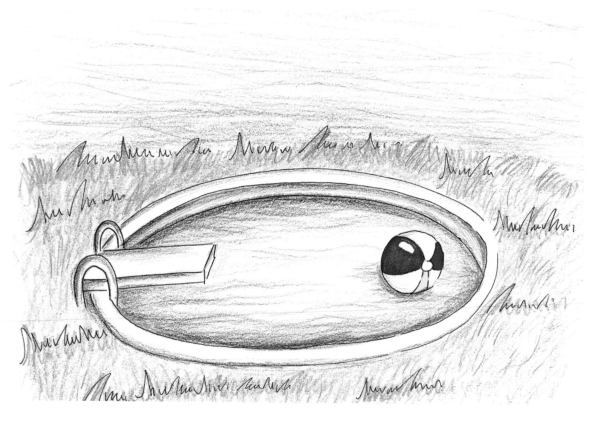

We'd play badminton, croquet and darts.

On the weekend we took bike rides to Belmont Lake and then walk all around the park and feed the ducks.

We loved going to plays and drive-in movies.

When we went for long car rides we'd sing songs or play "I see something" which is a guessing game.

Emily encouraged me to do my best at whatever I decided to try in life.

She supported me, believed in me and gave me confidence.

She showed me how to be a good person by being so loving and giving of herself. I was so blessed to have her as a role model of how to treat others.

She helped everyone in our neighborhood by sharing what she had grown in her garden, watching their children and baking everyone pies. Emily was a kind and generous soul.

Emily was also very creative. She made lovely clothes to wear. She also made beautiful outfits for my dolls. She designed and sewed costumes for me on different occasions.

She even made me coats to wear for holidays and special events. I was such a lucky girl to be Emily's daughter.

When I began to drive we became great travel companions. She enjoyed being my "co-pilot".

We took lots of road trips and I loved having her by my side. It was always more fun with my Mom along! We'd laugh and talk the whole way.

We'd usually bring food so we could stop by the roadside and have a picnic in good weather.

My mom and I would go for walks along the beach.

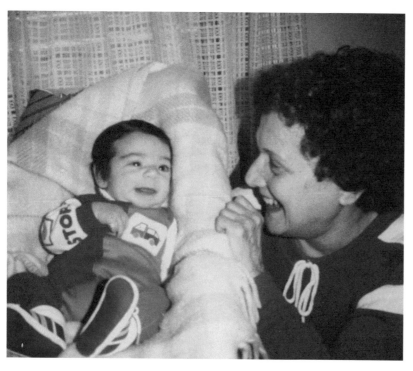

After I got married and had a baby, my Mom would take care of him when I went back to work. She enjoyed playing with my little son Sammy.

She'd make him super hero capes to play make believe games and climb trees with him like we used to do when I was little. She even taught him to swim.

They'd walk to the stores and she'd always get him a little toy.

She made his childhood as happy as she made mine and he loved her just as dearly.

Sammy didn't see his grandma as often when he went to school every day.

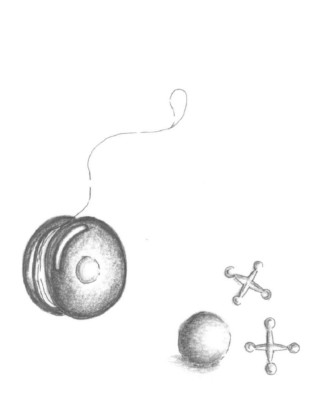

Emily had two pets to keep her company though. Her dog was a Beagle named Snooky and she also had a cat named Pookey.

Her pets would keep her from being too lonely when she missed seeing us.

As my mom was getting older, I would stop by to see her during the week. I noticed she would still be wearing the same sweater.

When I asked her why she didn't change she said, "because I like this sweater." It had a picture of a dog on it.

Then I noticed that my mom hadn't cleaned her house in a while. She used to be so neat.

When I asked her about it she said, "I'm not fussy anymore."

Other times when I visited I noticed she had burned some pots. She said she left something on the stove when she went in the backyard so all the water boiled out and evaporated.

I finally realised that my Mom was becoming so very forgetful that she might even burn her house down! So I began to feed her pets and take her home with me every night and bring her back after breakfast to spend time with her pets.

I'd stop by at lunch time to make sure she ate and pick her up again at night to have dinner and sleep at our house.

Each time we left her house she would ask me over and over again if we were going home. She recited her address at 108th street in Queens which is where she lived when *she* was a young child.

Then she would ask me who was going to take care of her dogs, "Dolly and Fanny?" These were the names of her pets when *she* was little, growing up.

In her mind, Emily was a little girl again, *not* my mom or Sammy's grandma.

Without realizing it, Emily would ask the same questions *over* and *over* and *over* again.

What made this happen is a disease of the mind called Alzheimer's. An older person can lose all recent memories and can only remember things from long ago. Not what happened last year, last month, last week or even yesterday.

In time as the disease gets worse, the person forgets how to take care of themselves. Then they need to be taken care of completely by someone else.

This is how I got to be Emily's caregiver as if I were her Mommy because she became like a little girl.

 I took my mom everywhere with me except when I worked. I used to bring her to a Day Care Center that cares for adults like my mom who have lost their memory.

At her program they had music and crafts for her to try.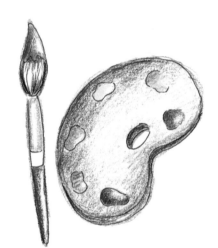

It was attached to a Children's Day Care Center so the adults could visit with the little children whom they really enjoyed!

At this point in time, my mother could no longer talk and only laughed. She was such a pleasure to be around because she was always happy. She still had the ability to enjoy everything around her.

She loved sitting and looking out the window at the birds and the squirrels. She could do this for hours.

At night she would sit on the couch with me and my husband and he would pat her knee. She enjoyed just being with our family.

After a few years, when she could no longer feed herself, I had to keep her home. So I hired a dear friend who always loved my mom to care for her while I was at work.

Since she had trouble swallowing I would make her delicious, nutritious smoothies and puree her food in a processor called the "Magic Bullet." Of course she also enjoyed ice cream and pudding.

To help her with balance I had a big walker for her to use around the house. By this time, my mom no longer made a sound and her face was expressionless.
She would sleep a lot.

My mom taught me how to be a nurturing caregiver by how she raised me with patience and love.

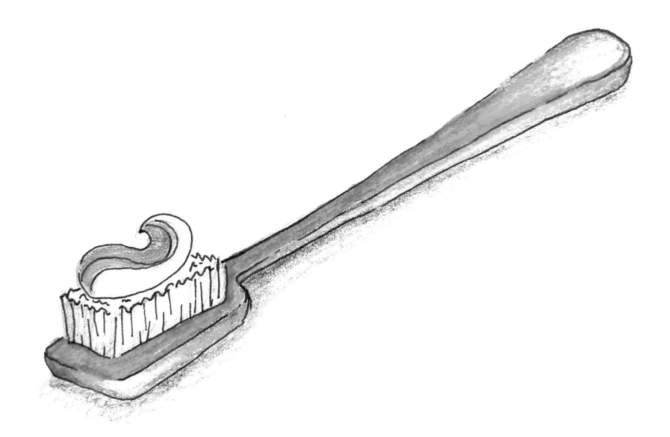

I enjoyed changing her diaper, bathing her, doing her hair, dressing her pretty, brushing her teeth and putting her to bed.

Caregiving is an act of love. I cherish that special time in her life that I was able to take care of the sweet, dear mother that so lovingly took care of me growing up.

Even though my Mom could no longer speak at the end of her lifetime, she watched me. Her eyes would follow me around the room. I know she was always looking for me...with eyes of love.

Dedicated to the precious memory
of my dear mother Emily.

I miss you so much Mom.
Thank you for everything!
Love,
Christine
xoxoxoxo